ST ANDREWS
CATHEDRAL

TEXT BY RICHARD FAWCETT

EDITED BY CHRIS TABRAHAM

DESIGNED BY POINTSIZE ASSOCIATES
PRINCIPAL PHOTOGRAPHY BY
DAVID HENRIE AND MIKE BROOKS

RECONSTRUCTION DRAWINGS
BY DAVID SIMON

PUBLISHED BY HISTORIC SCOTLAND

PRINTED IN SCOTLAND BY
HOWIE & SEATH LTD, EDINBURGH

ISBN 0 7480 0549 8

ST ANDREWS: A MEDIEVAL CATHEDRAL CITY

St Andrews was the focal point of the Scottish Church from at least the tenth century until the Reformation in 1560. During that time, many buildings were constructed and on a scale of magnificence unequalled anywhere else in Scotland. Fortunately, most of them survive today, in whole or in part.

At the very heart of the medieval cathedral city lay the **cathedral** itself, sited on a headland to the east of the burgh. Begun by Bishop Arnold about 1160, it grew to become the longest and greatest church in the land. Beside it a **priory** was built for the Augustinian Canons serving the cathedral. The great cathedral was built close by its predecessor, **St Rule's Church**, dominated by its lofty tower, and the whole sprawling cathedral complex was enclosed within a great **precinct wall**, the most impressive in

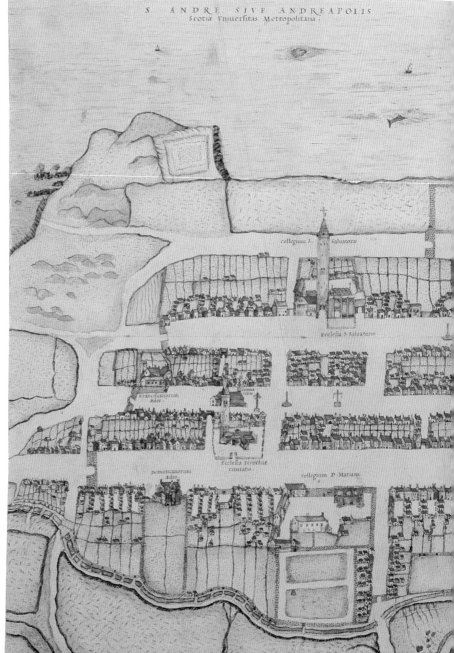

A sixteenth-century panoramic view of St Andrews (by permission of the Trustees of the National Library of Scotland).

Scotland. Immediately outwith the precinct wall, on the very edge of the promontory overlooking the harbour, lay the church of **St Mary on the Rock**, which probably occupies the site of one of the churches of the early religious settlement of Kilrimont (the old name for St Andrews) and where the successors of the Celtic monks were housed in the Middle Ages. To the north-west of the cathedral precinct was the bishops **castle**, situated on a strong cliff-top site. Elsewhere in the burgh is the **chapel of the Dominican Friars.**

All these buildings are now in the care of HISTORIC SCOTLAND and open to visitors and this fully illustrated booklet is a guide to their impressive remains. (There is a separate guidebook to St Andrews Castle.) A brief introduction to the early history of St Andrews prefaces descriptions of the buildings. These are treated separately so that each section serves as an individual guide.

The cathedral (page 10)

The priory (page 20)

St Rule's Church (page 8)

The precinct wall (page 24)

St Mary on the Rock (page 26)

The chapel of the Dominican Friars (page 27)

Saint Andrew and Saint Rule

Legend has it that Saint Rule (or Regulus) was the guardian of the relics of St Andrew at Patras in Greece in the fourth century. Warned by an angel that they were to be removed to Constantinople, Regulus resolved to take them elsewhere. Eventually his boat was wrecked off the Fife coast and the sacred bones of Saint Andrew were brought to Kilrimont and interred in a shrine.

It is an implausible story. If there were any relics of Saint Andrew here, they are more likely to have been brought by Bishop Acca of Hexham who was banished from his English diocese in 732 and apparently spent part of his exile in Pictland (that is, Scotland north of the Forth). Acca's predecessor at Hexham, Saint Wilfrid, was said to have acquired relics of the saint in Rome.

Saint Andrew, the patron saint of Scotland and of the cathedral, from an episcopal seal on display in the cathedral visitor centre.

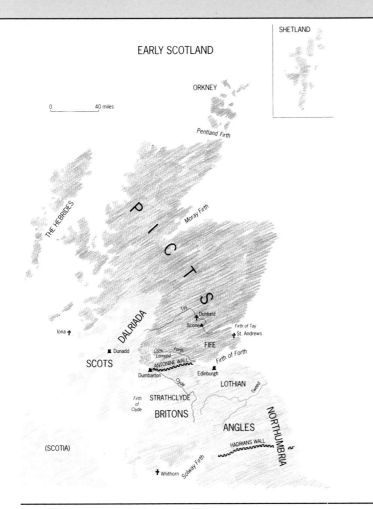

EARLY SCOTLAND

SHETLAND

ORKNEY

0   40 miles

Pentland Firth

THE HEBRIDES

P I C T S

Moray Firth

Iona ✝

DALRIADA

Dunadd ✝ Dunkeld
Scone ✝
Firth of Tay
St. Andrews ✝

FIFE

SCOTS

Loch Lomond   Forth
ANTONINE WALL
Dumbarton   Edinburgh
Firth of Forth

Firth of Clyde
STRATHCLYDE
BRITONS
Clyde

LOTHIAN
Tweed

ANGLES

NORTHUMBRIA

(SCOTIA)

HADRIANS WALL
✝ Whithorn   Solway Firth

OUT OF THE DARK AGES: KILRIMONT TO ST ANDREWS

In the Dark Ages, St Andrews was known as Kilrimont (Cillrigmonaid: 'church of the king's mount') but its early history is confused by later medieval attempts to give the Scottish Church a longer history than its English counterpart.

There was certainly a monastic community at St Andrews during the reign of Oengus, King of the Picts (probably Angus I, who ruled between about 729 and 761), for Irish annals record the death of its abbot in 747. The story becomes clearer by the tenth century. In 943 King Constantine II abdicated the throne in order to become leader of the monastic community. The brethren were 'vassals of God', Céli Dé (whence the name Culdees), a group of clergy who followed a very strict communal regime.

It may have been shortly before this time that Kilrimont became the headquarters of the Scottish Church. Iona's leadership had become impracticable because of persistent raids by Norsemen along the west coast and in 849 some of St Columba's relics were removed from there to Dunkeld, one of the centres of the united kingdoms of the Scots and Picts. This arrangement, however, proved unsuitable and by Constantine's time the community at Kilrimont, on a strong headland on the east coast, had risen to pre-eminence.

The Scottish Church was dominated by abbots, such as Constantine, who led the monastic communities, rather than by bishops responsible for defined geographical areas known as dioceses, which was generally the case in the rest of Europe. But from the tenth century we know there were chief bishops of the Scots, some of whom were probably based at Kilrimont.

The St Andrews Sarcophagus

The nature and sophistication of the sculpture from St Andrews demonstrates that the early Christian monastery had considerable support from a royalty with wide connections.

The St Andrews Sarcophagus, arguably the most important and certainly one of the most accomplished sculptures in Pictland, was found during grave-digging in 1833. Since then many further discoveries have been made and most of these are now on display in the cathedral visitor centre.

The so-called St Andrews Sarcophagus is a royal burial shrine of the late eighth century AD, perhaps a memorial to Oengus (died 761) of the powerful Pictish dynasty which founded St Andrews. It has nothing to do with St Andrew. Originally it probably stood inside a church to the left of the altar, the cross on its end facing the nave.

The shaft of a free-standing cross probably carved in the ninth century. One account of the monastery's foundation refers to the use of stone crosses to mark its boundary. Could this be the one?

The side panel of the Sarcophagus depicts a woodland hunting scene in which a mounted king attacks a lion. To the right, the biblical King David (identified by his ram and dog) defends his flock from a lion. The overall message is that heavenly salvation is obtainable through the right behaviour of kings who defend the faith. Its exotic appearance is deceptive because the composite box form, the designs and much of the repertoire is Pictish. However, the sculptor also had access to artistic models derived from the east mediterranean and near east (note the lions and monkeys). Ideas from these were successfully grafted onto native traditions.

The figures almost walk off the sculpture. This hunter follows his dog which is sniffing the trail of deer and wolves.

This house-shaped grave-marker originally stood in a long-cist cemetery over a ninth-century grave. Found in 1895 during building work at St Leonard's School, it implies the early monastery had several burial grounds and extended to the south of the later cathedral precinct. One foundation legend mentions seven churches.

The seal of Bishop Robert (1123-59).

Saint Andrew and Saint Margaret

In about 1070 Malcolm III married the Saxon Princess Margaret. By then the Scottish Church had fallen out of step with Church practice elsewhere in Europe, but Malcolm's deeply religious Queen started to bring it back into line. She founded a Benedictine priory at Dunfermline, the first in Scotland, and her devotion to Saint Andrew was shown when she provided the Queen's Ferry over the Forth for pilgrims to the shrine. She was later canonised as a Saint.

Margaret's sons built on her initiative. Her fifth son, Alexander I (1107-24), made three attempts to appoint bishops to Kilrimont to help him reform the Church. The first two proved unsuccessful. The third was Robert, Prior of Scone, the first Augustinian abbey established in Scotland in about 1120. Robert resolved to introduce a community of Augustinian Canons to make Kilrimont into a model cathedral foundation. As the cathedral chapter they would be responsible for

King Malcolm III and Queen Margaret, from the 16th-century Seton Armorial (by permission of Sir David Lindsay and the Trustees of the National Library of Scotland).

electing and advising the bishop and for providing services within the cathedral. Strong opposition from the existing clergy prevented Robert from achieving this until 1144.

When Robert became Bishop in 1123, there were at least two groups of clergy at Kilrimont, neither of which accepted responsibility for the main services of the cathedral. On the one hand there were the Culdees, numbering about thirteen; on the other were several independent priests. Both groups appear to have married, and neither group can have been viewed with favour by a reforming bishop.

Bishop Robert was determined that both groups would be superseded by the Augustinians, that all their endowments of land and wealth would be transferred to the new priory but that the Culdees would be given the opportunity to become canons. In the event they preferred to remain as a separate body, and they were eventually given a permanent home in the church of St Mary on the Rock. In about 1248, Bishop David de Bernham constituted them as a college of secular priests and thereafter they seem to have served as almost a rival cathedral chapter.

As the Culdee community faded into the background, so too did the Celtic place-name Kilrimont. The name St Andrews now came to be applied to Bishop Robert's new cathedral-priory and to the new burgh which he established in its shadow.

An Augustinian ('black') Canon dressed in his black habit (from Dugdale's Monasticon Anglicanum, 1655-73).

St Rule's Church, probably built by Bishop Robert soon after his consecration in 1127. The enormously tall tower (33m) was perhaps intended to draw pilgrims to the shrine of St Andrew.

ST RULE'S CHURCH

St Rule's Church as it might have looked in its final state. The church originally consisted of a tower rising to about 33 m with a rectangular chancel to its east and possibly another compartment beyond that. At a later date at least one more compartment was added to the east (since demolished) and a nave of unknown length added to the west side of the tower (also since removed).

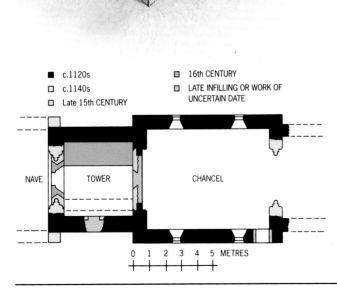

- ■ c.1120s
- □ c.1140s
- □ Late 15th CENTURY
- ▨ 16th CENTURY
- ▨ LATE INFILLING OR WORK OF UNCERTAIN DATE

NAVE   TOWER   CHANCEL

0 1 2 3 4 5 METRES

It was during the transition from Celtic Kilrimont to medieval St Andrews that the church of St Rule was built.

The dating of St Rule's Church is one of the great problems of Scottish medieval architectural history. Its plan is similar in some respects to a church found beneath the twelfth-century nave of Dunfermline Abbey. It is likely that part of that church was built for Queen Margaret. Some would like to see St Rule's as pre-twelfth-century, built during the time of Bishop Fothad, who officiated at the marriage of Margaret and Malcolm III at Dunfermline.

Although it could have been started earlier, most of the architecture of St Rule's appears likely to date from around 1130-50, during Bishop Robert's time. Before becoming Prior of Scone, Robert had been a canon at Nostell Priory, Scone's mother-house in Yorkshire. One of Nostell's dependent churches, Wharram-le-Street in north Yorkshire, has architectural details similar to those of two of the arches at St Rule's and it is possible that the same masons worked on both.

It seems likely, therefore, that most of what we see at St Rule's was built by Bishop Robert after his consecration in 1127, and that it was extended before 1144, by which time there was a better prospect of his introducing a chapter of Augustinian Canons. As a cathedral church it would have been very small by European standards but, from the little we know, it was one of the largest in Scotland for its time. It was only after Bishop Arnold, Robert's successor, started his vast new cathedral at St Andrews in the 1160s that the scale of Scottish cathedrals began to change.

The original tower and chancel, seen here from the south-west, are all that survive. They are built of massive blocks of finely-finished sandstone. The architecture is relatively simple, with a chamfered base-course around the bottom of the walls and a string-course (horizontal moulding) on corbels (projecting stones) at the level of the chancel wall head. This string-course runs around three sides of the tower clearly showing that the original intention was that the tower should stand at the west end of the church. The tower and chancel were linked by a high arch (now blocked). Lighting the chancel were two windows set high in each of its side walls.

The additions to east and west were probably carried out about 1144 to accommodate the Augustinian Canons. This lofty arch (now blocked) was cut through the west face of the tower to link the new nave with the original building. This arch is one of the details which shows similarities with the Yorkshire church of Wharram-le-Street. The nave was wider than the tower and was used by lay folk.

Detail of the secondary arch through the east end of the original chancel. Both this arch and the one cut through the west face of the tower are slightly more elaborate than the original tower arch and the slight irregularities in the stonework around their heads show that they were insertions.

The church was modified on later occasions, although its later uses are not known. The two tower arches were partly blocked and smaller doorways or arches inserted. The doorway in the east tower arch has the arms of Prior John Hepburn (1482-1522) above it. The tower was also heightened by a few courses about the same time, perhaps to provide a firm base for a timber spire. The west arch was further constricted by the present narrow sixteenth-century doorway, possibly when the stone spiral stair was inserted in the upper part of the tower.

St Rule's from the south-east. The arch through the east end of the original chancel was inserted to link with the eastward extension.

The cathedral from the tower of St Salvator's Church.

Like many great cathedrals, St Andrews was probably rarely without building works in progress, either to cater for changes in liturgical fashion or because of structural problems. The west end was blown down in the 1270s, and a century later, in 1378, a devastating fire raged through the building and major repairs were required. The faithful were encouraged to finance the repairs through indulgences, gifts which solicited assurances of reduced punishment for their sins. The rebuilding programme received a setback in 1409 when the gable of the south transept was blown down in a gale, damaging both the church and the adjacent domestic quarters.

THE BUILDING OF A NEW CATHEDRAL

Seal of Bishop Arnold, who founded the new cathedral following his election in 1160.

St Rule's Church soon proved too small for the chapter of Augustinian Canons and work began on a much grander cathedral. The project was started by Bishop Arnold shortly after 1160, with building operations concentrating on the eastern end containing the most important parts - the presbytery, with its high altar, and the choir, housing the canons' stalls. But the work took many years to complete. In 1202 Bishop Roger had to be buried in the old church of St Rule, because the new cathedral was insufficiently complete. His successor, William Malvoisin, was the first bishop to be buried there in 1238.

Much of the nave to the west was completed by the 1270s when William Wishart was bishop, though the mortar was hardly dry when the west front was blown down in a great gale. This front was then abandoned and rebuilt a little further back. The outbreak of the Wars of Independence with England in 1296 prevented consecration of the completed building until 5 July 1318, four years after Robert the Bruce's great victory at the Battle of Bannockburn, near Stirling. It was then carried out with great ceremony in the presence of the King.

This fine late medieval effigy of a mason, now in the cathedral visitor centre, was found in 1914 built into the north-east tower of the cathedral's precinct wall.

The ruined east gable of the new cathedral with the lofty tower of St Rule's beyond.

A thirteenth-century head of Christ, found during excavations at the cathedral in 1894 and now on display in the cathedral visitor centre.

11

The Eastern Limb

The eastern limb was eight bays long, and had an aisle on each side flanking all but the two easternmost bays. In most churches of this plan the presbytery containing the high altar projected east of the aisles. It is possible that at St Andrews this part housed the cathedral's relics, as was certainly the case by the later Middle Ages. The remainder of the eastern limb housed the canons' choir.

The east gable seen from the cloister.

The west wall of the south transept.

The Transepts

Projecting on each side of the west end of the choir was a transept (cross arm) of four bays, with an aisle of three chapels on their eastern side. Above the junction of the transepts and choir was a tower housing the cathedral bells.

N

The south wall of the nave looking towards the west front.

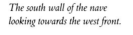

The reconstruction drawing shows the cathedral as it might have looked at the time of its consecration in 1318.

The cathedral was laid out on a variant of the cross-shaped plan usual for a major church, with the more sacred parts towards the east.

The Nave

West of the transepts was the long aisled nave, which was accessible to the lay folk and eventually came to house a large number of altars. It was originally designed to consist of fourteen bays but it was reduced to twelve following the collapse of the west front in the 1270s.

The west doorway.

Entrances

There were several entrances into the cathedral. The great ceremonial entrance was at the centre of the west front, but the main entrance for the lay folk was on the north side of the nave where it was eventually sheltered by a porch. A number of doorways were provided for the canons from the priory on the south side of the church. Two doorways aligned with the walkways of the cloister gave access to the nave and were used for processions. A third doorway in the south transept connected with the staircase from their dormitory, and there may also have been a fourth door in the north transept leading to the cemetery.

THE EASTERN LIMB

Building work on the cathedral began at the eastern end so that the most important parts of the church were ready for use first. Only parts of this eastern limb survive, but one of these is the east gable, and there is enough of the rest to understand how the whole would have appeared.

St Andrews Cathedral is a landmark in the architectural change from Romanesque to Gothic in Scotland and northern England, as well as being influential in passing on some of the new ideas which had been introduced into northern England by the Cistercian order of monks from its first home in eastern France. Many features of its design seem to have provided an inspiration for monastic churches elsewhere, like Jedburgh and Arbroath in Scotland, and Hexham and Lanercost in northern England.

The east gable from the south west.

Originally the gable had three tiers of three windows. The upper tiers were later replaced by a single large window, after the fire of 1378, but the outlines of the first windows can still be seen. Gables like this had been used in the great Romanesque churches since at least the early twelfth century and were especially popular with the Cistercians, who liked their simplicity.

The stumps of the side walls can be seen projecting westward from the gable. At this point they were not typical of the rest because the flanking aisles did not start until further west. Nevertheless, the relative proportions they indicate, together with the fragments of piers separating the choir aisles from the choir itself, show that the design was of three storeys, as was usual in larger churches.

The refurbishment of the eastern limb following the fire of 1378 also resulted in the floor being raised by several steps to create an elevated relic chamber. The large tombstone marking the raised floor has been moved slightly eastwards to reveal three stone coffins beneath.

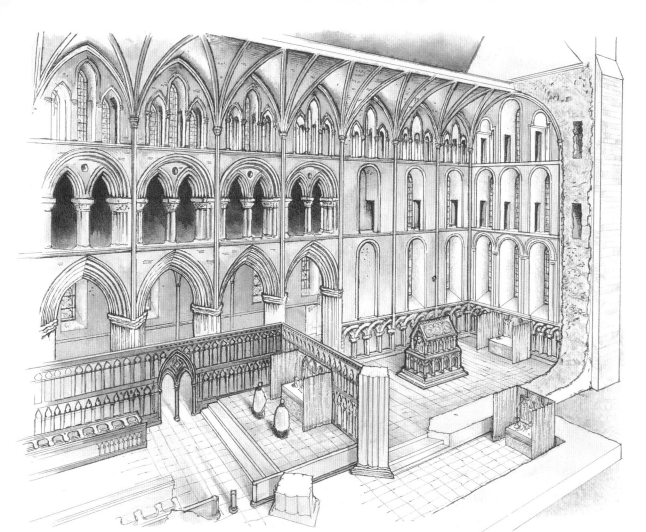

The stone head of Bishop Henry Wardlaw, now on display in the cathedral visitor centre along with other elements from his effigy and tomb. Bishop Wardlaw was buried on the north side of the presbytery in 1440.

The eastern limb as it might have looked when first completed.

The side walls, like the east gable, were divided into three stages, although there were differences of design between those parts flanked by aisles and those parts without.

The lowest stage comprised an arcade of arches carried on tall piers opening into the flanking aisles. Above was a high gallery within the roof space over the aisle vaults, probably with a single arch in each bay embracing two smaller arches. (In the eastern bays the two lower storeys had windows rather than open arches, since there were no flanking aisles.) At the top was a clearstorey, which rose up into the stone vaulting covering the eastern limb. The clearstorey was a tier of windows lighting the central space and set behind a passage in the thickness of the wall.

Many of the details of this design show the influence of the Cistercians. In particular, the piers were made up of bundles of eight shafts, and the capitals decorated with fleshy foliage known as water leaf.

The choir stalls, where the canons sang their services, extended down the two sides west of the presbytery. They would have been screened off from the part of the church open to lay folk.

THE NAVE

Although the eastern bays of the nave were built along with the choir to provide support for the tower, the construction of the rest followed the completion of work on the eastern limb. It was nearing completion only in the 1270s, over a century after work began. During the course of these protracted building operations, architectural fashions changed and developments of design can be detected in the nave.

The original west front stood two bays further west but was blown down in the 1270s. The existing west front is its replacement. This was intended as a great show-piece, with a magnificent doorway of five receding orders of arches flanked by tall polygonal turrets marking the line of the nave arcades. At first the new front had a vaulted porch stretching across it, up to the height of the nave aisles, and the lines of the vaulting ribs are still visible.

The upper part of the west front was rebuilt after the great fire of 1378. Two tiers of windows (one only survives) above a row of decorative arcading were inserted and handsomely-proportioned pinnacles added to the turrets. The porch was probably removed at the same time.

The design of the windows, inserted after the fire of 1378, with triangular groupings of three circlets, suggests an early example of French architectural influence. It is not known which bishop paid for the windows but Bishop Landallis (died in 1385) had been

appointed at the request of the French King, and Bishop Trail (died in 1401) had been educated at the university in Paris. Either bishop knew France well enough to have introduced the idea at a time when relations with England were again poor.

The south aisle wall of the nave from the cloister.

This wall gives the clearest indication of a change in architectural style (from Romanesque to Gothic) inevitable in such a protracted building operation. The most obvious change is in the design of the windows which pass from the simple, round-headed shape to the wider, pointed form with Y-tracery.

The impressive west front.

The celebration of Low Mass, depicted in a late fifteenth-century miniature belonging to Archbishop Alexander Stewart (by permission of the Trustees of the National Library of Scotland).

The illustration shows what some of the lesser altars of the cathedral would have looked like. The canons followed the psalmist in praising God seven times daily in services known as the canonical hours. These 'hours', eventually numbering eight, began very early in the morning with Nocturns and Matins, continued with Prime, Terce, Sext and None, and finished in the evening with Vespers and Compline. Each consisted of psalms, prayers, anthems and readings. In addition, mass for the community was celebrated at least twice a day, and individual canons would also say private masses. After the earlier of the two community masses, the morrow mass, the canons met in the chapter house next to the church to confess their faults and discuss business matters.

The cathedral was the setting for many functions. It was the church within which Scotland's most important bishop had his *cathedra* (seat), the symbol of his authority in sacred matters. It was the mother-church of the bishop's diocese. It was also a major centre of pilgrimage. But its most intensive use was for the daily worship of the canons (the cathedral chapter) who were responsible for providing a continuous offering of prayers and praise.

The seal of the cathedral chapter (13th century).

In 1418, the cathedral prior was permitted to wear the mitre by the Pope. This gave him the same status as the bishop. Because of St Andrews' position as the senior diocese of the Scottish Church, the prior took precedence over the heads of all the other religious houses. Technically, the prior and canons had the right of electing the bishop, but in practice it was the Pope and later the King who made the choice. By the Reformation (1560) even the prior was chosen by the King.

KEY	
☐ DUNKELD	◼ ST. ANDREWS
◼ CAITHNESS	☐ DUNBLANE
☐ ROSS	☐ GLASGOW
☐ MORAY	☐ GALLOWAY
◼ ARGYLL	☐ SODOR
☐ BRECHIN	◼ ABERDEEN

The extent of the diocese of St Andrews.

In addition to their cathedral duties, the canons may have taken some interest in the parish churches - nearly thirty in all scattered throughout the diocese - from which the cathedral-priory drew much of its income. The nearby church of Leuchars (pictured here), the finest Romanesque church in Fife, was granted to the canons by Nes, Lord of Lochore, about 1185. The canons tended also to have intellectual interests, and it was in the priory dining hall in 1414 that the Pope's letters establishing the new university of St Andrews were read out.

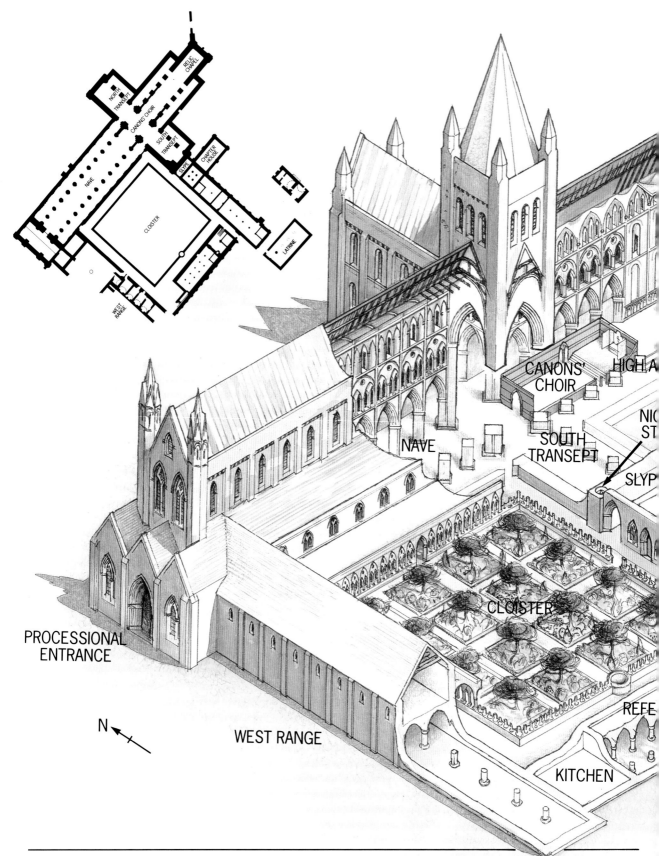

NORTH TRANSEPT

RELIC CHAPEL

CANONS CHOIR

SOUTH TRANSEPT

SLYPE

CHAPTER HOUSE

NAVE

CLOISTER

LATRINE

WEST RANGE

CANONS' CHOIR

HIGH A

NAVE

SOUTH TRANSEPT

NIC ST

SLYP

CLOISTER

PROCESSIONAL ENTRANCE

N

WEST RANGE

REFE

KITCHEN

THE CATHEDRAL PRIORY

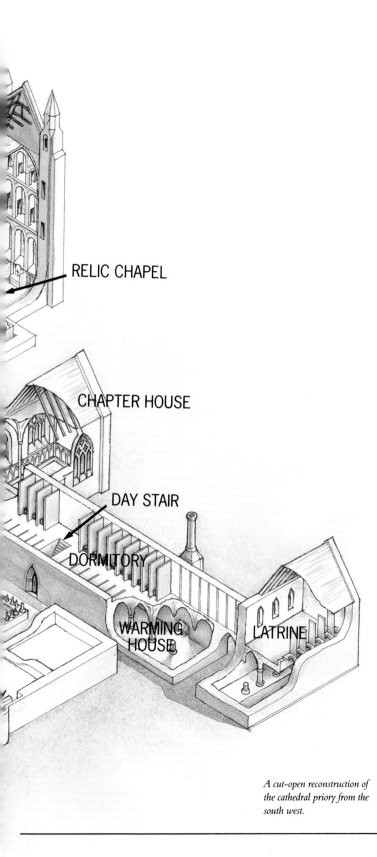

RELIC CHAPEL

CHAPTER HOUSE

DAY STAIR

DORMITORY

WARMING HOUSE

LATRINE

A cut-open reconstruction of the cathedral priory from the south west.

The domestic quarters of the Augustinian Canons were to the south of the cathedral where they could gain the maximum sunlight. The nucleus, containing the chapter house, or business room, the dormitory and dining hall, was arranged around a square open cloister. Beyond lay the wide range of other buildings required by such a wealthy and complex institution. These included an infirmary for sick and elderly canons, a residence for the prior, guest halls, byres, barns and granaries. There were even other churches, including the chapel of St Mary Magdalen and the old parish church of Holy Trinity, which stood to the east of the cathedral until it was superseded in about 1410 by a new building in South Street. The sprawling precinct covering over 12 hectares was enclosed by a strong wall through which were several gateways.

Not everything was built at once, of course, and throughout the Middle Ages there was continual change. Surviving records show that the dormitory, dining hall and guest hall were completed during Prior John White's time (1236-58). Prior John of Haddington added a hall for the prior's residence in about 1270. Bishop William Lamberton rebuilt the chapter house in time for the burial therein of Prior John of Forfar in 1321. This and other rebuilding may have been necessitated by the destruction caused by the English King, Edward I, in 1304 early on in the Wars of Independence. This included the stripping of lead from the roofs to make artillery shot.

Other alterations were made as a result of age and changes in fashion. These included the building of an imposing new main gateway into the precinct, the Pends Gate to the west of the priory, probably in the late fourteenth century, and the heightening of the walls and projecting towers in the time of Prior John Hepburn (1482-1522).

THE PRIORY BUILDINGS

The priory buildings are now largely represented by low wall foundations but sufficient survives for us to understand the layout. Some parts were rebuilt by Lord Bute in the 1890s. In order to identify his work he used red sandstone, a stone quite unlike any used in the medieval building, and he had his masons identify their work with masons' marks.

The decorative arcading in the cathedral wall at the north end of the west cloister range indicates that a building of some importance once stood here.

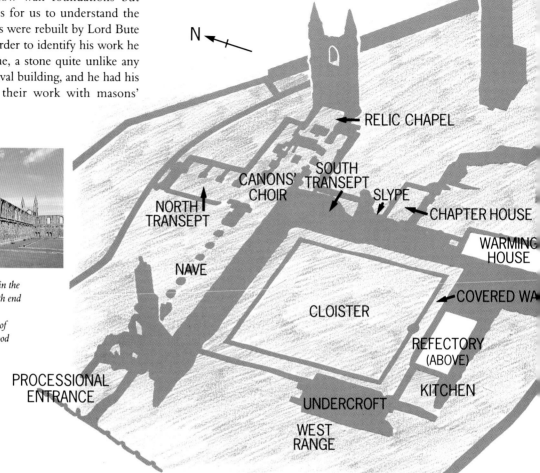

ST RULE'S CHURCH

N

RELIC CHAPEL

CANONS' CHOIR

SOUTH TRANSEPT

SLYPE

CHAPTER HOUSE

NORTH TRANSEPT

WARMING HOUSE

NAVE

CLOISTER

COVERED WA

REFECTORY (ABOVE)

PROCESSIONAL ENTRANCE

UNDERCROFT

KITCHEN

WEST RANGE

The West Cloister Range

The **west cloister range** was put to a variety of uses down the years and the buildings there were modified several times. At the south end is a vaulted **undercroft** in which the cellarer may have kept the priory's provisions. In their present state they appear to date from the sixteenth century. The rooms above were reached by both an internal

and an external stair and judging by the much modified entrance doorway must have been of some importance. Perhaps they were the residence of the sub-prior, the second-in-command, who is recorded as living in this area.

Later on the 'senzie house' was here. This may have been the consistory court, where the

Church heard legal cases over which it had jurisdiction.

The range became wider where it adjoined the church. Whatever was next to the church at the upper level must have been of importance judging by the elaborate thirteenth-century decorative arcading which runs along the wall.

The undercroft in the west cloister range.

The East Cloister Range

The **east cloister range** contained several important rooms. The **slype** was a passage leading from the cloister to the buildings beyond. There are book cupboards in the transept wall.

The doorway into the slype, with St Rule's Church beyond.

The chapter house.

The **chapter house**, the main business room, was rebuilt in the early fourteenth century. It has a vestibule within the range, but the meeting room itself projected beyond to allow the room to be more lofty. The canons sat on arched seats around the walls. Those on the south side still survive. The chapter house was a favourite burial place for priors, and several stone coffins have been exposed beneath its floor.

The rest of the **undercroft** was divided into various rooms, including the warming house, where the canons warmed themselves in cold weather. Part of it was reconstructed in the 1890s and now contains the primary display of carved stones found at the cathedral over the years.

On the upper floor was the **dormitory**. This was originally a long open room but in time the individual beds were separated by partitions.

Leading from the dormitory directly into the cathedral was the **night stair**, for use at night-time services. Originally this was a narrow spiral stair but it was later replaced by a straight flight. There was also a day stair leading down into the cloister; this was probably entered through the doorway towards the south end of the range.

At the south end of the dormitory was the **latrine**. The drain, still visible, is built of smooth stone so that waste matter flowed freely away.

The South Cloister Range

In the **south cloister range** the main building was the **refectory** or dining hall. It was carried on a vaulted undercroft which was reconstructed in the 1890s. This now houses the visitor centre and secondary display of the cathedral museum. The large dining hall itself was above the main section of the undercroft. To the east at first-floor level was a small room apparently used to store precious vestments, perhaps because its proximity to the warming house made it warm and dry. To the west of the dining hall were the **kitchens**.

The vaulted undercroft in the south cloister range, reconstructed by Lord Bute in the 1890s.

ATRINE

THE PRECINCT WALL AND PENDS GATE

Prior John Hepburn's coat-of-arms dated 1520, on display in the cathedral visitor centre.

The surviving part of the precinct wall begins at the north-east corner of the cathedral and sweeps round the east and south sides to a section on the south-west side which has been re-aligned in modern times. Thirteen towers survive and four gateways, including the main gateway, known as the Pends Gate, and a gateway known as the Teinds Gate where the canons received the teinds, or dues from their numerous parishes which provided the greater part of their income.

This precinct wall is the most imposing in Scotland.

The upper parts of the wall date from the time of Prior John Hepburn (died in 1522) and his nephew, Patrick, who succeeded him until his elevation to the Bishopric of Moray in 1538. Prior John's coat-of-arms is displayed on the towers and gates. But the Pends Gate indicates that there had been an earlier wall, and certainly the lower part of the wall on the north-east appears to be of earlier date.

A typical tower along the precinct wall.

An image niche on one of the towers.

The Pends Gate, the main gateway into the precinct.

The fine blind arcading above the outer arch is so similar to that designed for the west front of the cathedral after the fire of 1378 (see page 16) that this gateway may also be of that date. The gates themselves were between the first and second bays from this north side.

THE CHURCH OF ST MARY ON THE ROCK

Modern excavations around St Mary's revealed over 300 early Christian burials of all sexes and ages. That some individuals were commemorated by grave-markers is indicated by the many ninth- or tenth-century cross-slabs that have been found on the cathedral headland.

St Mary on the Rock from the top of St Rule's Church.

To the east of the cathedral, on the promontory overlooking the harbour, are the remains of the church of St Mary on the Rock (also known as St Mary Kirkheugh). Although outside the precinct wall, its site was probably one of the most ancient parts of Kilrimont. Many of the early cross-slabs in the cathedral visitor centre were found here in 1860, during the construction of a coastal defence battery.

The Culdee monks who refused to join the cathedral priory were given the church here, and in 1248-49 their successors became the first college of secular priests in Scotland. The college enjoyed the protection of both kings and bishops, and from about 1290 until perhaps as late as 1501 it was regarded as a Chapel Royal. In 1385 its leader, the provost, was allowed a place in the cathedral choir and chapter, which cannot have pleased the Augustinian Canons who probably regarded the college as a rival establishment. By the Reformation in 1560 there were at least thirteen clergy, known as prebendaries, in the college.

Their church was an aisleless cross-shaped building, with a choir longer than the nave and transepts of uncertain length. There are signs in the stonework of at least three building phases, of which that in the nave seems the earliest. The finest masonry is in the eastern part of the choir, which was probably extended at some stage to house the prebendaries in a more spacious style.

At the east end of the choir is the high altar base, and a projection from the south wall may have belonged to seats (*sedilia*) where the officiating clergy sat during parts of the mass. A door on the opposite side could have led to the sacristy, where the priests robed and where precious items might be safely stored. There may have been a small tower over the central crossing. South of the church is a reconstructed stretch of wall with a doorway, perhaps a fragment of the accommodation for the clergy, or the house of their provost.

THE CHAPEL OF THE DOMINICAN FRIARS

At the western end of South Street is the ruin of another ecclesiastical building. It is the only surviving fragment of the Dominican Friary, founded in the burgh sometime in the fifteenth century.

The Dominican Friars, known as Blackfriars from the colour of their habit, saw one of their roles as rooting out heresy and they tended to be associated with centres of learning, where they could develop their intellectual skills. It was probably the foundation of the university in the burgh in 1410 which attracted them to St Andrews.

In the early sixteenth century the Scottish Dominicans experienced a revival and in 1516 it was agreed that money bequeathed to them by Bishop Elphinstone of Aberdeen should be devoted to new buildings in St Andrews.

The surviving fragment is a side chapel which originally projected from the north side of their church. It could date from after 1525 when permission was given for the friars to build out into the street because there was insufficient space in their own grounds.

The chapel, polygonal in shape, has large traceried windows in four of its sides with the fifth left blank to accommodate an altar with its carved or painted altarpiece. The windows, though heavily restored, suggest Dutch influence in their simple loop-like forms; the stone-vaulted ceiling is typically Scottish. The junctions of the cross ribs have carved bosses, one with the symbols of Christ's Passion and the other with the arms of Hepburn (perhaps a reference either to Dean George Hepburn of Dunkeld who supervised the building work, or to Prior John Hepburn of the cathedral priory).

THE CATHEDRAL AND THE REFORMATION

One of many fine post-Reformation tombstones now on display in the cathedral visitor centre.

The Reformation of the Scottish Church in August 1560 had a devastating effect on the cathedral priory and the other churches in the town. By then, much of the damage had been done for the turning point proved to be a sermon preached by John Knox in the parish church on 11 June 1559, which so aroused the congregation that they were immediately moved to tear down the rich medieval furnishings associated with 'popish' worship.

At the cathedral, which was still staffed by over thirty canons, the Archbishop seems to have accepted the inevitable. The great church was abandoned virtually immediately since the parish church was sufficient for his reduced needs. The roofs were stripped and the building that was once Scotland's most splendid church was reduced to a stone quarry. Lord James Stewart, Commendator (lay administrator) of the priory in place of the prior, continued to live in part of the canons' cloister for some years after, but by 1597 the priory buildings were in decay.

The college of St Mary on the Rock, which still had thirteen clergy attached to it in 1559, was also extensively damaged in June of that year and it must have been shortly after this that many of its buildings were demolished.

The Dominican Friars were a particular target of the Reformers, perhaps because they represented the 'intellectual' wing of the old

Church. That they occupied prime building land in the burgh may have contributed towards their vulnerability to attack. The friary had been attacked in 1547, but the main onslaught took place on 14 June 1559 and a week later it was reported that all remaining friars had been violently expelled. The friary land was immediately granted to the burgesses and it is unlikely to have been long before the buildings were reduced to the small fragment we now see.

During the reigns of James VI (1567-1625) and Charles I (1625-1649), there were times when it seemed that the cathedral would have a new lease of life. Both kings had lived in England since 1603, had come to prefer the forms of worship they found there and were always anxious to strengthen the hand of the bishops against the growing clamour for their removal. As late as 1634 Charles I had called for a report on the feasibility of restoring the cathedral.

But it was not to be. The Scottish people were not favourably disposed to a monarch whom they suspected of 'popish' leanings and who had visited the country of his birth only once since becoming King of Scots. In 1638 the office of bishop was abolished and, although Charles II restored it in 1661, it was finally abolished by William of Orange in 1689. Deprived of any function, the cathedral fell rapidly into decay.

John Knox preaching from the pulpit; a 19th-century stained glass window in St Giles, Edinburgh.

The cathedral ruins from the north at the end of the seventeenth century (illustration by Captain John Slezer).

The cathedral precinct as it might have looked about 1550 (illustration by Alan Sorrell).

The Bishops and Archbishops of St Andrews

(Only those bishops who appear actually to have governed the diocese are included)

Maelduin	?c.1028-1055
Tuthald	?1055
Fothad	c.1070-1093
Turgot	c.1107-1115
Robert	1123-1159
Arnold	1160-1162
Richard	1163-1178
John Scot	1178-1188
Roger	1189-1202
William Malvoisin	1202-1238
David de Bernham	1239-1253
Abel de Golin	1254
Gamelin	1255-1271
William Wishart	1271-1279
William Fraser	1279-1297
William Lamberton	1297-1328
James Ben	1328-1332
William Landallis	1342-1385
Walter Trail	1385-1401
Henry Wardlaw	1403-1440
James Kennedy	1440-1465
Patrick Graham	1465-1478
(created Archbishop 1472)	
William Scheves	1478-1497
James Stewart	1497-1504
Alexander Stewart	1504-1513
Andrew Forman	1514-1521
James Beaton	1521-1539
David Beaton	1539-1546
John Hamilton	1546-1571
John Douglas	1571-1574
Patrick Adamson	1575-1592

Episcopacy abolished in 1592, but existing bishops allowed to remain in place. Bishop Gledstanes of Caithness translated to St Andrews in 1604 but consecrated Archbishop only in 1610 on revival of episcopacy in 1610.

George Gledstanes	1604-1615
John Spottiswood	1615-1638

Episcopacy again abolished in 1638. Revived in 1661.

James Sharp	1661-1679
Alexander Burnet	1679-1684
Arthur Ross	1684-1689

THE CATHEDRAL TODAY

More than 400 years have elapsed since the Reformation of 1560 and tempers have long since cooled! They had cooled sufficiently by the end of the eighteenth century for the burgh's great medieval buildings to be appreciated once more. Repairs were undertaken to St Rule's Church in 1789 and in 1826 the Barons of the Exchequer accepted responsibility for the cathedral. In 1946 the priory was given to the State by Major M D D Crichton-Stuart.

Today the medieval streets of St Andrews are filled with visitors coming to enjoy the golf, the fine beaches and the marvellous atmosphere of this thriving university town. Of Scotland's ancient burghs, St Andrews most of all has retained its medieval heart and soul, thanks in large measure to the survival of its once-mighty cathedral, its attendant priory, the lofty tower of St Rule's Church and the other ancient monuments cared for by HISTORIC SCOTLAND.

The memorial to "Tommy" Morris, the renowned golfer, in the cathedral graveyard.

IN MEMORY OF
"TOMMY"
SON OF THOMAS MORRIS
WHO DIED 25TH DECEMBER 1875 AGED 24 YEARS

DEEPLY REGRETTED BY NUMEROUS FRIENDS AND ALL GOLFERS
HE THRICE IN SUCCESSION WON THE CHAMPION'S BELT
AND HELD IT WITHOUT RIVALRY AND YET WITHOUT ENVY
HIS MANY AMIABLE QUALITIES
BEING NO LESS ACKNOWLEDGED THAN HIS GOLFING ACHIEVEMENTS

THIS MONUMENT HAS BEEN ERECTED
BY CONTRIBUTIONS FROM SIXTY GOLFING SOCIETIES

Further Reading

J Dowden
The Bishops of Scotland (1912)

I Cowan & D Easson
Medieval Religious Houses: Scotland (1976)

D McRobert (ed)
The Medieval Church of St Andrews (1976)

R Fawcett
Scottish Cathedrals (1997)

S Foster (ed)
The St Andrews Sarcophagus (1998)

J Gifford
The Buildings of Scotland: Fife (1988)

A Ritchie
Picts (1989)